The Communication Toolkit

For a complete list of Management Books 2000 titles
visit our web-site on http://www.mb2000.com

Other books in this series include:

The Customer Service Toolkit
The Developing People Toolkit
The Human Resources Toolkit
The Learning Toolkit
The Motivation Toolkit
The Systems Thinking Toolkit
The Team Management Toolkit

The Communication Toolkit
Practical ways to improve personal and work performance

Stuart Emmett

2000

This book is dedicated to my family – to my wife, the lovely Christine, to our two cute children, Jill and James, and James's wife, Mairead (also cute), and to our totally gorgeous three granddaughters, twins Megan and Molly and their younger sister, Niamh.

First published in 2008 by Management Books 2000 Ltd
Forge House, Limes Road
Kemble, Cirencester
Gloucestershire, GL7 6AD, UK
Tel: 0044 (0) 1285 771441
Fax: 0044 (0) 1285 771055
Email: info@mb2000.com
Web: www.mb2000.com

British Library Cataloguing in Publication Data is available

ISBN 9781852525637

Contents

About this book

In writing this book, I have made best-efforts endeavours not to include anything that, if used, would be injurious or cause financial loss to the user. The user is, however, strongly recommended, before applying or using any of the contents, to check and verify their own company policy/requirements. No liability will be accepted for the use of any of the contents.

It can also happen in a lifetime of learning and meeting people, that the original source of an idea or information has been forgotten. If I have actually omitted in this book to give anyone credit they are due, I do apologise and hope they will make contact so I can correct the omission in future editions.

About the author

My own journey to "today", whilst an individual one, did not happen, thankfully, without other people's involvement. I smile when I remember so many helpful people. So to anyone who has ever had contact with me, then please be assured you will have contributed to my own learning, growing and developing.

After spending over 30 years in commercial private sector service industries, I entered the logistics and supply chain people development business. After nine years as a Director of Training, I then choose to become a freelance independent mentor/coach, trainer and consultant. This built on my past operational and strategic experience - gained in the UK and Nigeria - and my particular interest in the "people issues" of management processes.

Trading under the name of Learn and Change Limited, I currently enjoy working all over the UK and also on four other continents, principally in Africa and the Middle East, but also in the Far East and South America. In addition to my training activities, I am also involved in one-to-one coaching/mentoring, consulting, writing, assessing and examining for professional institutes' and university qualifications.

I can be contacted at stuart@learnandchange.com or by visiting www.learnandchange.com. I welcome any comments.

Preface

Welcome to this new series of business toolkits designed to improve personal and work performance.

A recent report entitled "The Missing Millions – how companies mismanage their most valuable resource" (source: www.Proudfootconsulting.com) stated that "Poor management in the UK is directly responsible for 60 lost working days per employee per year. And a further 25 days lost annually can also be indirectly attributed to management failing."

That is a total of 85 wasted days per employee every year due to poor and failing management. This is around 30% of a normal working year of 240 available days!

According to the report, the main contributing factors were as follows:

- Insufficient planning and control
- Inadequate supervision
- Poor morale
- Inappropriate people development
- IT related problems
- Ineffective communication

This series of concise guides will provide practical advice in each of these key management areas, to enable managers to get the most out of their teams, and make sure that they stay ahead of the game.

The simple truth is that in order to avoid the incredible 85 wasted days per employee per year referred to above, things must be done better *by management.*

Problems with management will almost always turn out to be people problems. Improving performance is therefore essentially about improving individual and team performance so that, in turn, the organisation's performance is improved.

This will require that, for example, the following are considered:

- Developing a strong strategic vision that is underpinned with learning
- Motivating and developing and releasing the potential of people, as individuals and in teams
- Communicating to people what is expected, what they are rewarded for, how they should deliver results and what results the organisation is looking for.

The earlier mentioned Proudfoot research highlighted several areas that managers can work on to improve performance. These are shown again below with a link to the appropriate Toolkit:

- Insufficient planning and control – see the Systems Thinking Toolkit
- Inadequate supervision – see the Team Management Toolkit
- Poor morale – see the Motivation Toolkit
- Inappropriate people development – see the Developing People Toolkit
- IT related problems – see the Systems Thinking Toolkit
- Ineffective communication – dealt with in this Communication Toolkit

It should be appreciated that many of these aspects do inter-relate, and that a single quick fix in one area may not always work very well. The Systems Thinking Toolkit does examine more fully all of the interconnected links of inputs, processes and outputs to be considered when improving performance. Also, the Learning Toolkit is paramount, as improvements can only be made after making changes and change, in turn, is directly associated to new learning.

As we have seen, many of the Proudfoot research aspects are directly people-related. In addition to the specific toolkits mentioned above, the Human Resources Toolkit provides a complete framework for effective human resources management.

Finally, as we all know, no business can survive without customers, and the essential skills of customer service are absolutely vital to the retention and growth of the customer base. The Customer Service Toolkit provides quick and easy advice which will produce startling returns.

Part 1. The Communication Problem

Communication is an aspect of management that is constantly complained about by employees. It represents a major barrier to improving performance.

It is arguably one the most important management skills, yet whilst it seems it will always be imperfect, it is also something that can be continually improved.

Polls regularly uncover a critical shortage of communication skills among managers. For example, in ILM Edge December 2006 the law firm Eversheds reported that "the overwhelming majority of workers (97%) are calling for their bosses to communicate more clearly".

Definition of communication

Communication has been variously defined as:

- "Sharing information between people"
- "Exchanging of ideas that require a reaction"
- "The sending and receiving of verbal and non verbal messages"
- "The art of being understood"
- "The prevention of misunderstanding"

It takes two to communicate; it is a two-way process. Effective communication also involves feedback and the testing of understanding.

One-way telling, for example, is not very effective communicating; nor are the "communication boards" of one large UK PLC which shall remain nameless (the boards were simply notice boards with a new name).

Communication is an active and not a passive process. It involves sharing and exchanging with active involvement between people. As NLP practitioners have noted, the meaning of communication is in its effect. Communication must always have a result.

Communication, ideally, should always be as clear, direct, short and simple as possible. If it is important enough, then it should be done in person as this enables the use of varied communication methods with reinforcement and repetition.

Problems with communication

Communication is a two-way process that most people, however, only attempt to do one way (mistakenly believing they have communicated). As communication is two-way, then it must have both a sender and a receiver. However the two players are often poorly connected; and their skills are often weak both in the sending and the receiving of communication.

Professional communicators, like those in media, advertising and PR, are always consciously striving to get a message across to others. The rest of us are less aware of the process. We must work harder to improve our communication.

Distractions/barriers that limit our communication

Consider please the following diagram:

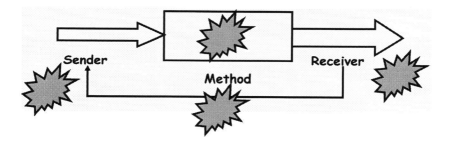

This shows very simply, that problems in communication can arise in many places; in the sender, in the method used, in the receiver and in the feedback.

One theory of communication (Shannon and Weaver) identifies six separate stages that must exist for communication to be effective. At each of these stages there may be barriers to communication.

1. **Conceiving the Message**. Consider the content of the message. What is the purpose? What do you intend should happen as a result? The message should be clear, concise and accurate.

    Barriers: The sender may not be clear. Irrelevant detail may disguise the intended message. Information may be inaccurate or expressed in vague ambiguous terms.

2. **Encoding the Message**. Always consider the needs of the receiver by choosing the most appropriate 'language'. The style, vocabulary and manner of presentation may actually convey as much as the message itself. Different vocabularies and styles will therefore suit different purposes, e.g. formal instructions or advice, requests or simply information.

   Barriers: If the wrong style is used, the wrong level of priority may be given. Also, the wrong language or vocabulary (jargon, etc.) may result in misunderstanding.

3. **Selecting the Medium**. Different messages require different mediums – oral face to face, or oral by telephone, written reports, memos, pictures or diagrams. The need for speed, confidentiality and/or a written record, the complexity of the message and the number of receivers will all influence the choice of the medium to be used.

   Barriers: The complexity of the message may be unsuited to some mediums (e.g. giving directions by telephone). The volume of written communication may result in overload with important messages being overlooked. Oral instructions may be unheard, or misheard due to physical barriers such as noise.

4. **Decoding the Message**. The receiver decodes the message according to their own understanding of the vocabulary used.

   Barriers: Specialist jargon may be misunderstood by non-specialists. Some people cannot read or they may have reading difficulties.

5. **Interpreting the Message.** People are complex. They read between the lines and interpret messages (often incorrectly) according to their relationship with the sender, or based on the past experience of similar situations, or based on the attitudes and culture.

   Barriers: Poorly conceived messages that are ambiguous are likely to be misinterpreted. Wrong assumptions may be made when instructions are not explicit. A classic example is the sign "authorised persons only beyond this point". Who is and isn't authorised? Culture and past experience may create a perceived difference between what is said and what is meant. Expectation can play a part, too, as people may hear what they expect to hear and jump to conclusions.

6. **Feedback.** Unless the sender is provided with prompt, unambiguous feedback, communication errors cannot be corrected. Feedback, therefore, whether it is it written, oral or visual (with signals and body language), is an important form of communication. Some mediums allow feedback more easily than others. Notice boards, for example, are unlikely to produce any feedback, apart from unintended graffiti. Lack of feedback is in itself a barrier to communication.

17

Perception as a barrier

Differences in perception can dramatically affect the way we see things, as the following well-known picture illustrates.

People, who look at this picture, will see two very different ladies.

Some, will see an older women (the front three quarter view and wearing a head scarf), yet others will see a young lady (the side rear view and wearing a plume in the hair).

What this shows is that we have different behaviour and thought patterns, and these can influence what we see (or hear).

What we see and hear is very real to us. However, this reality may not, be the one, the sender intended we experience.

"Feelings are facts," is another expression, which suggests that what we think about, and have feelings about, represents our view of the "reality" of the facts. Again, the perceived reality may not be the one which was intended by the sender.

Attitudes as a barrier

Consider please the following diagram:

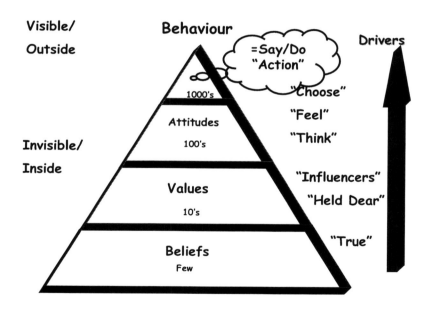

Our attitudes, underpinned by our beliefs and values, will work through into how we behave (defined here as what we say or do).

We all therefore tend to judge from our perspective alone and we may not always consider fully the other parties involved – these being the sender, or, the receiver/the audience.

When communication "has gone wrong", we can all be very quick to identify the failings in these other parties, rather, than in ourselves.

Behavioural style as a barrier

Our behaviour has its own "style" that can be

- Aggressive
- Passive
- Assertive

In their extreme forms these types of behaviours may be characterised as follows:

Autocratic and aggressive: hard positional negotiator

- drives and pushes people but is not a leader
- has a single "my" viewpoint
- one-way communicator
- demanding ("do it my way, now")
- takes fixed "my-way" positions
- prone to a contest of will
- makes threats and applies pressure

Procrastinator and passive: soft positional negotiator

- abdicates from taking decisions
- uses group viewpoints
- is indecisive, claiming to be "democratic"
- "what do you all want to do?" (and when?)
- changes positions easily
- avoids any contest
- makes offers and yields to pressure

Charismatic and assertive: partnership negotiator

- pulls more than pushes
- two-way communicator
- a leader who people follow naturally
- makes concessions, "I think this... what do we think?"
- solves problems and explores interests
- reasons, and encourages partnership views
- looks for objective criteria and yields to principles not pressure

For those that recall the 1970s BBC TV series "Dad's Army", autocrats are like Captain Mainwaring and procrastinators are like Sergeant Wilson

The out-working of these styles is seen in the specific behaviour used, as follows:

Trait	Passive Behaviour	Aggressive Behaviour
View of Self	Inferior to others	Superior to others
Feelings	Fear, nervy, tense	Domineering, demanding, anger
When under Pressure	Retreats	Attacks
Self Esteem	Puts self down as is dependant on what others think	Others are put down, their views are insignificant

The above patterns of behaviour actually represent basic animal instincts; for example, the aggressive male lion and the passive submissive lioness.

A more human characteristic is assertive behaviour that is not instinctive. This sees "self" and others as being more or less the same. Assertive people accept themselves and other people, warts and all.

Assertive people know what they want and can ask for it in a way that does not damage their own self-esteem or the other person's.

They feel comfortable and self-confident with others and in control of the situations they face. They solve problems rather than point score; they look for win/win.

Assertiveness is somewhat important, and therefore, we shall return to it later.

Other barriers in communication

There are three other types of barriers in communication: personal barriers, process barriers and organisational barriers.

Personal barriers can be seen as follows:

- Inappropriate management style
- Inconsistency as a communicator
- Incorrect timing
- Not being seen as credible – for example, you are not believed/trusted
- Not making sure the target audience is interested and ready to receive the message
- Not knowing where to go for answers to your people's questions
- Not understanding your responsibilities and those of others
- Not having good working relationships with colleagues

Process barriers are briefly as follows:

- Channels may be inappropriate, e.g. appearance, voice tone, body language, rank/status, etc.
- Loading, e.g. overloading/swamping
- Feedback is blocked, therefore communication is no longer two-way
- Questions are asked, but no answers expected

Organisational barriers are briefly as follows:

- Company culture: the levels of consultation, conflicts, decisions, meetings, power, rewards, pace of work, etc.
- Physical environment: resources, space, comfort, etc.
- Organisation size: people normally expect that smaller organisations will be better at communicating than their larger counterparts, but this by no means always the case.

Overcoming barriers in communication

How can we overcome the above barriers? Getting answers to the following questions will help:

General questions to ask

- What is the most acknowledged failure?
- What can I do about it?
- What do I want to do about it?
- Who else should be involved?
- What is the cause?
- Determine measurable improvements
- Plan for the next time
- Check and review

Specific questions for your Section/Department

- Is there evidence of an interchange of ideas?
- Do your employees know the reasons for the job they are being asked to do?
- Can you introduce changes without major upsets?

- Do you use ideas put forward?
- Do you explain why you cannot use ideas put forward?
- Do you consult with those nearest to the job on matters affecting them?
- Do you induct new employees carefully?
- Do all your people know what their jobs are?
- Do your people show a sustained interest in their jobs?
- Do you walk round at least once a day?

Specific Questions to ask in the Organisation

- Is there a smooth flow of work "either side"?
- Do you consult with specialists within the company?
- Do you deal with problems without having to refer them?
- Are you ever bypassed in the flow of information?
- Is the "grapevine" large or small? (Note that the grapevine is an ever present and ever active conveyor of facts and bad news, but mainly rumour – by feeding it, you can influence it, but you can never control it.)

Potential false assumptions in communication

Communicators often make false assumptions which can lead to problems or failures of communication. Here are three common examples:

1. Comments made are intended to be harmless, yet they may cause problems and annoyance to others.
2. Comments made are bold, yet they may cause offence.
3. We assume others are listening, when they are not.

The first two examples are complicated as the problems hinge on the beliefs and attitudes of the receivers. However, this emphasises the need to check understanding, so that any such anomalies can be highlighted, discussed and hopefully corrected.

In the third case, it is obvious that it takes two to communicate and if the other party will not do play their part (by listening), then all we can do is explain what was our intention and ensure that we have done all we can to try to prevent the misunderstanding.

Listening

Hearing and listening are not the same yet we often hear people say "you did not listen", "I am speaking but you are not listening" etc. etc. Again this is a two-sided issue, and it presents some special issues that we will now examine.

Listening is not easy. Consider the following chart comparing the way in which listening, speaking, reading and writing are respectively learnt, taught and used,

	Listening	Speaking	Reading	Writing
Learnt	1st	2nd	3rd	4th
Taught	4th if at all	3rd	2nd	1st
Used	1st (50%)	2nd (30%)	3rd (15%)	4th (5%)

This is somewhat sobering as listening is used a lot but we are rarely taught how to do it; although I am sure many of us can remember being punished at school for not listening!

However we do learn to listen very early as a child; after all, our speaking skills developed from listening to others speak.

Listening is also a crucial aspect of personal relationships which is constantly mentioned by counsellors dealing with marital problems, where a common complaint by the wife is "he does not listen to me." The emphasis on the lack of male listening is, I have to say, usually confirmed by the women who have attended my training classes; this is irrespective of nationality/ culture etc. It does seem widespread that men are poor listeners.

The following sayings may be of assistance, (especially to male readers)

- **"You have two ears and one mouth. Use them in that proportion."**

- **"The mouth is designed to close; your ears are not."**

- **"To answer the question before you have heard it is stupid."**

- **"If you enjoy listening, then you are a good learner."**

- **"Be quick to listen but be slow with your answer."**

- **"Listening with the inner ear helps you to understand the inner person."**

When listening to someone speaking to you, it is important not to instantly "jump in" with comments. We must pause and reflect and consider what has been said, by working on the facts and not our "instant" assumptions, which come from our prejudicial attitudes.

We have all witnessed, for example, a conversation where one person cuts in with something to say, before the other person has finished speaking. When the response is given in the same way, we then quickly see an escalation towards heated voice tones. Then, the discussion turns into an angry confrontation.

Listening is very important, but a surprisingly rare skill. We will return later on to the question of how we can improve our listening.

Part 2. Communication and Management

Communication is like the baton in a relay race; it has to be passed on.

Criticality of communication

If management is about getting things done with people, then communication is a critical aspect of any manager's job.

To plan, organise, direct and control work activity – all of these rely to a greater or lesser degree on effective communication. Communication failures can therefore be very expensive, as the wrong things can get done. To avoid these problems, *direct* communication is the most effective way to ensure that people know/ understand /act as is intended.

Employees will also need to know how they are performing. For example, overhearing someone say, "I think I am doing OK, as I have not been sacked yet" is just not good and is reflective of ineffective feedback communication. Additionally, employees should be told how the organisation is performing, even when they do not ask.

This requirement to involve others takes time and effort. Often, it involves not just "telling," but requires more "selling", with both talking and listening. Excluding others, when they actually have something they want to contribute, will send its own message.

Communication is therefore an important part of the manager's job.

In the very early stages of the development of a business the owner deals directly with the staff. The owner is personally interested in them as individuals, knowing and making allowances for them and their problems, limitations, and special aptitudes.

Later as the business grows, the owner becomes removed from the staff owing to other management and business preoccupations, and managers are appointed to control each department; the owner of the business has now delegated to the managers the personal contact and the exchange of opinions, feelings and information.

Some of these managers will look at the elaborate communication network in their organisations. They might see, for example, a company magazine and the company notice board and conclude: "I don't need to bother with communication myself as top management is communicating direct".

These managers forget that you cannot discuss with a magazine, bulletin, or notice board and that some may read the wrong message between the lines. These methods of communication are just not personal enough. There is no opportunity for question and answer. The expression on the other person's face cannot be seen. Never forget that body language is a vital ingredient to effective communication.

Key management responsibility

The manager should be the direct personal link between the staff and top management. Managers have a clear responsibility to communicate downwards, as well as upwards.

Communicating Downwards

Managers must interpret policy decisions and actions to their staff. If managers actually disagree with the policies, then they may say so to their manager, but this disagreement is not for publication.

Managers should obtain and pass on enough information about the job, the department and the company to enable their people to work intelligently and with the enthusiasm which comes of knowing what the work is for. If senior management does not volunteer much information, managers should not wait to be told but must ask.

There are five main methods of keeping staff in the picture:

1. Make sure that new staff receive a proper briefing when joining the company.

2. Ensure that they know their terms of reference and targets and their progress in achieving them.

3. Make a point of having daily contact with every member of staff, in order to:
    - set standards (tidiness, safety, personal appearance, punctuality, conducts, etc.)
    - show appreciation
    - give constructive criticism or guidance where needed
    - ask if there are questions or problems and sort them out

4. Call the occasional staff meeting to pass on information you may have received from your superior, explain plans and

31

impending changes or review past performance as a basis for your future intentions.

5. Ensure that any formal newsletters or notice boards are kept up to date.

Communicating Upwards

All managers are interested in two main items, the staff and the work.

Therefore managers should keep their own boss informed about people's problems, feelings, reactions and ideas.   In companies where managers leave this to others, then these others will spend too much of their time making up for management's own poor communication. It is perhaps therefore understandable if these others then go on to start trying to run the department.

What should you tell your manager about the work and its progress? They need enough information about what you are doing so as to ensure that they will never are taken by surprise concerning duties and responsibilities which have been allocated to you.

The main classifications of information the boss needs from you are as follows:

*   Progress on Long-Term Work. Periodic reports, monthly or quarterly, should keep them briefed on how any major project is developing.
*   Exceptional Events. Using the "Management by Exception" principle means only reporting when there is something significant to say.

32

- Deviation from Plan. For example, a job is scheduled for completion on 1st May, but you are behind, because two of the staff has been away sick and one of your suppliers was late with a delivery. It is important to let the boss know this, so that he (or she) can take steps to speed the job up further along the line, warn the customer, and perhaps call in outside help. Others rely on you, to tell them the facts, however unpleasant.
- Anticipated Problems. You are often better able to foresee problems than others, so make sure your boss is warned in time to take action.
- Suggestions about Work Method Changes. Choose the right time to broach the subject and support the idea with facts and figures. Think through the snags and find the answers to any possible objections, so that the idea does not have to be shelved pending further information being obtained.

Assertive communication

This can perhaps be seen as a management style, a philosophy of personal responsibility and an awareness of the rights of other people. It will involve being honest with yourself and others, by having the ability to say directly what it is you want, what you need or how you feel, but not doing any of this, at the expense of other people.

Assertiveness is therefore having self-confidence and being positive, while at the same time understanding other people's points of view and being able to negotiate and reach workable compromises.

Assertiveness is not easy

In both philosophy and action assertiveness is simple. The reality for most people is that we all have both culture and gender behaviours that mould us into particular reactions and types of behaviour.

For example, men are encouraged from birth to:

- be tough
- be strong
- be in control
- not back down
- give as good as you get
- show no weakness
- win if you can, never mind the cost

Women, on the other hand, are encouraged from birth to:

- be gentle
- to follow
- be compassionate
- put others before herself
- to share
- not to argue
- not to get angry

Culture too has a part to play in preventing assertiveness from being easy. In some countries bartering, even arguing, is a way of life. In others, like Britain, queuing up and waiting patiently for your turn is the order of the day.

How to be assertive – a quick view

- Actively listen to what is being said, and then show the other person that you both hear and understand them. This will force you to focus on the other person, and not use the time they are talking to build up a defence or attack. By really listening, you are able to demonstrate some understanding and empathy for their situation or point of view, even if you do not wholly agree with it.
- Say what you think or what you feel. This enables you to directly state your thoughts or feelings without insistence or apology.
- Say what you want to happen. This is essential, so that you can indicate in a clear and straightforward way, what action or outcome you want, without hesitancy or insistence.

Assertive and communication

The rules which follow are general but are comprehensive. However, assertiveness is not about using a series of quick fix tricks or techniques. It is also not a way to manipulate and manage other people so that you get your own way, while looking as though you are considering others.

The guidelines are not, given in any significant order.

Rules for being assertive

- **Be clear about what you want; if you don't know what you want, then you will find it difficult to communicate your wishes and needs to others.**

- Choose your time and place; choose the most appropriate place to communicate and a time when the other person can listen. If necessary, delay the discussion (even if only for a few seconds) until you can give the matter your full attention.

- Make a clear statement; it may help to rehearse your statement. Don't allow yourself to become upset or to lose track of what you want to say.

- Be specific; get straight to the point and identify clearly, and directly, what you want or what you want to convey.

- Express what you feel; it sometimes helps to say that you feel anxious, happy or angry when making a statement, request or a response. But say it only once and then return to the point.

- Do not be side-tracked; if the person you are talking to tries to side-track, then listen to what is said but repeat your own point. Do this again if necessary.

- Give reasons, not excuses; it is better to give reasons than excuses for what you want or don't want to do.

- Be prepared to compromise; think about your 'fallback position' before you start to communicate; when you have expressed your feelings, be prepared to agree an outcome which everyone can accept.

The effective communicating manager is brief and clear, and knows what has to be said, about what, to whom and why. They will always consider the receiver, (for example, their expectations, openness and readiness for communication), but they do know that they cannot control the receiver's interpretation.

Communication flows

Communication needs to flow easily between people. The following "ideal-typical" diagram illustrates this, starting with the initial tone of the communication, then the general direction taken, and finally the result.

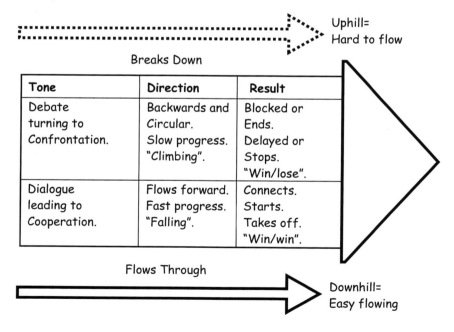

Uphill=
Hard to flow

Breaks Down

Tone	Direction	Result
Debate turning to Confrontation.	Backwards and Circular. Slow progress. "Climbing".	Blocked or Ends. Delayed or Stops. "Win/lose".
Dialogue leading to Cooperation.	Flows forward. Fast progress. "Falling".	Connects. Starts. Takes off. "Win/win".

Flows Through

Downhill=
Easy flowing

The tone and direction of effective communication is analogous to water flowing downhill where natural gravity helps. Ineffective communication is analogous to water flowing uphill; it is an uphill struggle.

Just as individuals can work on their communication flow, so can teams as a whole. For a discussion of the dynamics of teamwork in communication, see the Team Management Toolkit.

Part 3. Effective Communication

Key factors

Albert Mehrabian, Emeritus Professor at UCLA, assessed the key communication factors as follows:

Key factors	Effectiveness
Content- What is said - The Words	7%
Style - How we speak- The Voice Tone	13%
Body Language – How we look	80%

Mehrabian's research deals primarily with messages about feelings and attitudes – for example, when people say they like or dislike something in a face-to-face communication. (When communicating "plain" facts, the effectiveness rating of content would obviously take precedence.)

On the basis of Mehrabian's ratings, it follows that if someone says they like something, but their voice tone and body language are not in congruence with the words, then the words will not be believed.

However, what is also somewhat sobering about this listing is its implications for communication by phone or in writing, when the key factors in communicating feelings face to face are lost. Body language can only be used effectively when we are physically present, actually "eyeballing" the people we are trying to communicate with.

Body language and voice tone are important on both sides of the communication. We need to "receive" non-verbal communication as well as impart it. We all know how difficult it can be speaking on the telephone to someone we have never met in person. On the phone, we at least have the words and voice tone to help us form a view of the person we are speaking to. With email and other forms of written communication, we only have the words. Interestingly, when we finally meet this person who we have phoned or emailed, the view and opinion we had of them can change dramatically when we are "face to face." Often they will appear completely different from how we had imagined them. For example, terse, cold and direct words are actually, coming from a smiling friendly and warm face.

Here it is the body language that has come from the visual contact which makes a difference in our perception.

> **"I need to see the business leaders' body language and the passion they poured into their arguments".**
>
> **(Source: Jack Welsh)**

When communicating face to face, the body language may be what people will "believe." This is being communicated and is a part of giving the understanding and meaning in the message.

It is important, therefore, to actively consider the most appropriate methods of communication. Whilst our everyday methods of communication remain largely the same, the tools do change. For example, the recent use of email changes the "mix" and is also, as discussed below, often used inappropriately.

Communication methods

The following listing will assist on advantages and disadvantages of some commonly used communication methods.

Verbal communication

e.g. meetings, telephone, etc.

Advantages

- Direct, no time lags
- Immediate feedback
- Allows for discussions
- When face to face, uses the potential power of effective body language
- Quick

Disadvantages

- Often used unplanned, acting in haste without thought
- Forgetting vital information
- "Chinese whispers" that distort messages as they are passed on
- Not confidential
- Poor retention, especially if the information is complex

Written communication

e.g. email, letters

Advantages

- Permanent record
- Convey complex information
- Identical message to many

Disadvantages

- Time and cost
- Time lag between sending and receiving
- Used to avoid face to face contact
- Easy to copy in many other people meaning many others can receive "pointless" messages
- No real opportunity to test understanding

Visual communication

e.g. fax, TV, histograms

Advantages

- Reinforces verbal messages
- Gives extra stimuli
- Simplifies words
- Illustrates

Disadvantages

- Time and cost
- Interpretation
- Design skills
- No real opportunity to test understanding

All of these methods can be combined, for example:

- Verbal explanations, followed by written instructions
- Written reports, followed by a meeting to discuss
- Visual flowcharts, followed by written procedures

Email communication

Email has become the cause of many communication breakdowns and conflicts. Perhaps no surprise, for as we saw earlier, words can have a low effectiveness ranking in some communications.

Effective uses of email are in conveying clear facts and asking yes/no questions about those facts. Email is useful to provide or request for information and agreeing simple plans, like meeting dates, times, locations, etc.

However, whilst email can compensate for the absence of face-to-face communication, it should never be seen as a replacement for it when, for example, feelings need to be communicated. Indeed, some organisations have now chosen on one day a week to prevent internal email in their offices, so that people are readily encouraged to talk face to face.

Advantages of email

- Speed
- Accessible by all on a worldwide basis
- Access to information via the web
- Rapid transmission of files/documents

Dangers of email

- Overloading
- Needs total clarity on words
- Receivers may use their delete button, so sending an email does not mean the message has been understood or has been acted on
- Using the technology to replace human contact

Body language

As intimated earlier, body language can represent the "secret" signals of behaviour that go far beyond the meaning given from just simple words and voice tone.

Eye contact is the number one aspect of body language as the eyes are "the lamp of the body" that reveals the inner self; eye contact shows our interest and concern in the other person.

There are also many other aspects of body language, for example:

- Head movements, e.g. nodding/shaking
- Gestures "speak" a lot, e.g. smiling, finger pointing
- Posture , e.g. slouching, shrugging, leaning
- Breathing, e.g. snoring, anger
- Touching, e.g. closeness, friendly

All of these aspects and features can be combined, for example:

- Passive = little eye contact, slouching, sullen, etc.
- Aggressive = fixed eye contact, lean forward, finger pointing, etc.
- Receptive = friendly "crinkled eyes", relaxed, smiling, etc..

Meanwhile, the following listing shows what is communicated to others by our body language:

Body language	Assertive	Aggressive	Passive
Posture	Upright / straight	Leaning forward	Shrinking back
Head	Firm not rigid	Chin jutting out	Head down
Eyes	Direct not staring good and regular eye contact	Strongly focused staring, often piercing or glaring eye contact	Glancing away. Little eye contact
Face	Expression fits the words	Set, firm	Smiling even when upset
Voice	Well modulated to fit content	Loud, emphatic	Hesitant, soft, trailing off at ends of words or sentences
Arms/ Hands	Relaxed, moving easily	Controlled extreme/sharp gestures, finger pointing, jabbing	Aimless, still
Movement/ Walking	Measured pace suitable to action	Slow and heavy or fast, deliberate, hard	Slow and hesitant or fast and jerky

Communication techniques

In this section, we will discuss the following basic communication techniques:

- Listening
- Questioning
- Giving and receiving feedback
- Presenting
- Report writing
- Meetings

Listening

Listening is an important skill to develop. Listening is not just the natural and passive act of hearing. Listening is more about understanding and then going on to act on what has been heard. (A Chinese proverb says "I hear and I forget, but I do and I understand").

We can listen negatively and there are many ways this can be done;

- **Emotional listening**: The sender's powerful emotion causes an emotional reaction in the receiver that blinds them to what is actually being said.
- **Dismissive listening**: The listener quickly decides that the speaker has to say will not be worth listening to. Dismissive listening is common when someone is being given bad news.
- **Destructive listening**: Similar to dismissive listening, but here the listener is only intent on putting down the

46

speaker with a destructive power play. Politicians frequently do this; so do people who have racial or cultural prejudices.

- **Judgmental listening**: Jumping to incorrect conclusions.
- **Distracted listening**: This comes from trying to do two or more things at once and not giving any one of them your full attention.
- **Submissive listening**: The listener thinks of the speaker as powerful, wonderful, or aloof. Pop stars and sports heroes are often given this kind of attention.
- **Anxious listening**: This happens when you are so anxious that you hear little of what is being said. Often important information from medical consultants or lawyers can be missed due to anxiety.
- **Apathetic listening**: Sometimes you may feel bored, apathetic or even contemptuous. Usually there is a deep-seated fear behind apathy.

Listening is not therefore an easy skill to learn. Yet, its importance is immense. How many times has someone criticised us for not listening?

Listening is hard work, which requires concentration. We need to be Active Listeners.

Here is the problem: most people think about four times as fast as they speak, so each listener has about 75 per cent of each listening minute spare. This spare time is often then used on "own" business.

Concentration demands interest, so any new input must then battle for attention.

One "trick" to help is to behave in a way implies concentration – thus, for example, by being prepared and acting interested and involved, this will improve our ability to concentrate. So don't wait to be "in the mood"; get started and act interested. Often enthusiasm will grow out of our action.

Active Listening in a one-to-one situation involves us looking the other person straight in the eye whilst they are speaking. Listen without interrupting. Absorb what they say, and try really to understand. When they have finished, repeat it back to them by paraphrasing what was said. For example, "so as I understand it, what you said is X". Only when they agree, can you move forward. This shows that we have listened and demonstrates we have heard.

Active and Productive listening in a group situation, starts by understanding ourselves and then by understanding the listening situation.

Let's expand this further:

1. Get Ready

- Review what you expect, (for example, the notes from any previous meeting).
- Eliminate any distractions (for example, uninterested colleagues).
- Anticipate what is being said as you then become active.
- Determine why you are there so you know why you are listening.
- You are there complete, not just the body, but with an active mind to focus on the now and not on yesterdays or tomorrow problems.

2. Assume the position

- Sit up, don't slouch, let your posture speak.
- Watch, as well, as listen, to body language, to visual aids, etc.
- Acknowledge what you hear by nods and questions; your active involvement completes a positive feedback loop to the speaker.
- Take notes.
- Squarely face the speaker
- Open posture is to be kept by you, as this shows the speaker you are receptive.
- Lean slightly forward, as this shows your presence and interest
- Eye contact holds interest.
- Relaxing shows you are at ease and receptive.

3. During the process

- Focus on content and ideas and believe what the person is saying is true for them. Do not focus on their appearance/accent/tone/personality. Focus on why you are there – for example, to gain or refine knowledge or skills. Focus your attention as you would if you were having a one-to-one conversation with a close friend.
- Abbreviate your notes. It is you who need to understand them, not anyone else. Also abbreviate your own ideas so you can understand the speaker's ideas!
- Review and revise your notes within 15/20 minutes of the end.

So "**READY–SWAT/SOLER–FAR**" is the mnemonic for listening. (Mnemonics, even complicated ones like this, can be a helpful memory aid!)

Questioning

To paraphrase Peter Drucker, the problem with most Western managers is their emphasis on trying to find the right answer, rather than asking the right question. It is important, therefore, to ask challenging, positive but constructive questions.

There are seven types of questions that can be used to achieve understanding and encourage appropriate action.

You might also find that asking yourself some of these is quite a challenge:

1. Help to find or make meaning

- What does this mean to you?
- What is this saying to you?
- Can you see a pattern or a theme in all this?

2. Encourage others to learn from the past

- Has this happened before?
- Give me some examples of incidents like this in the past?
- How did you tackle similar situations, and what happened?

3. Show that you are caring and supportive

- How do you feel?
- What would help you right now?
- You've done harder things than this before, what's different about this?

4. Seek practical examples or illustrations

- What sort of things are you talking about?

- Can you give examples of other situations in which you feel this way?
- Who else do you know that has had this issue?

5. Look to the future

- What will happen if you do that?
- What obstacles are there?
- What resources will this require?
- Where do you want to be with this in six months' time?

6. Initiating action

- How do your action plans fit together?
- What alternatives and options do you have?
- What is the best next step?
- What do you want to do about this?

7. Balancing and moving on

- Can you see a trend linking past, present and future?
- So, what you seem to be saying is..?
- Can you summarise the actions you're going to take?

Types of questions

All questions are either "open" or "closed". **Open questions** require an open response; they are also exploratory questions – for example, "Could you tell more about your marriage?"

Closed questions will tend to signify the response required, often a yes or no – for example, "Are you married?"

Here are a number of different types of question which can be useful:

- **Directive/closed** e.g. "Don't you need to do this?"
- **Informative/open** e.g. "How will you deal with the problems I myself encountered?"
- **Confronting/open** e.g. "Why did you get angry?", or "What is it that is keeping you awake at the moment?"
- **Cathartic/open** e.g. "How do you feel?" or "Where in your life do you feel the most stuck at the moment?"
- **Analytic/open** e.g. "Will you go into detail?" or "What are the 10 things that are stopping you at the moment?"
- **Supportive/closed** e.g. "You did well, didn't you?", (very important and gives enormous benefit, to used as much as genuinely possible!)

"Open" questions are usually the most important ones to use as "closed" questions have very limited and specific uses.

Questions to establish rapport

Similarity, for example

- What opinions do we share?
- How much are we the "same"?

Control, for example

- How much does each of us like to control?
- How will we all share control (learner over content, helper over process?)

Supporting, for example

- How will we behave in a nurturing way to each other?
- Will this be a two-way process?

Emotional, for example

- Can we be spontaneous?
- How shall we show our real emotions and let each know how we really feel?

Confidentiality, for example

- How shall we ensure confidentiality'?

Problem-solving, for example

- How best can we work together in a logical manner to solve problems and make decisions?

Co-operation, for example

- How will we co-operate?
- What are our previous experiences of co-operating like?
- How flexible can we be?

Challenge, for example

- How can we challenge each other so that we can achieve positive conflict and positive compliance?

Cosiness, for example

- How will we stop our meeting becoming only a cosy place for a chat "just for the sake of it"?

Conflict, for example

- Do we both fully understand about conflict?
- How will we avoid spending valuable time in any destructive arguments (negative conflict)?
- How will we ensure we have time for open and constructive disagreement and discussions (positive conflict)?

Compliance, for example

- How will we both commit to achieve positive compliance and not "just go along with things" (negative compliance)?

Presenting

A simple approach to presentations

- Plan the main points you want to say
- Order the main points
- Structure the presentation as follows:
  - Introduction (very short with the main theme)
  - Reasons for listening ("Sell")
  - Teaser (Map the journey)
  - Content (Main part)
  - Summary (Roundup of the main points)
  - Conclusion (What do they need to remember)
  - Ask if there are any questions?
- Speak clearly, firmly, without shouting
- Use visuals as appropriate
- Rehearse the body language
- Make a maximum of three points at a time
- Engage the audience

A detailed approach to presentations

Plan

- What is your general aim?
- What are your specific objectives?
- What are your main points?
- Are these expressed in active terms?
- Can they be achieved in the time available?
- How many are in the audience?
- Who are they?
- What do they already know?
- What are their specific interests?
- What approach will they better respond to?
- What do you already know about the content?
- How can you find out more?

Preparation

- Have you prepared an outline?
- Is it logical?
- Is it understandable?
- Is it too vague?
- Can it be shortened and still make sense?
- How will you get the audience's attention?
- What will they expect?
- What is in for them?
- Will it help to them to visualise or to see your words?
- What about any supporting material?
- Is it relevant?
- What visual sides will you use?
- Are they simple?
- Can they be seen?

- Are you sure you will be saying what you mean?
- Is a written summary appropriate as a handout?

Practice

- Will you practice before the event?
- Is the presentation a part of you?

Presentation

- Be there early
- Check the room, equipment, etc. that you will be using
- Make the audience active
- Control the questions
- Emphasise the main points
- Give summaries of the main points, throughout the presentation
- Give a final summary of all of your main points, at the end
- Test and check understanding
- Enjoy
- Afterwards, think/reflect and learn/improve for the next time

Report Writing

Every report has a writer, a subject, a purpose, and a reader. Therefore the first stage must be to ask:

- What is the purpose?
- Who are my readers?
- What will influence them?
- What do they need to know?
- Will they understand my terminology?
- What will prevent them understanding the report?

During writing be consistent about the form layout and numbering and the style and language.

Structure

The overall structure is as follows:

1) Title page and Contents
2) Introduction
3) Summary of recommendations
4) Present situation
5) Analysis
6) Recommendations/Conclusions
7) Appendices
8) Acknowledgements/References/Bibliography
9) Index

1) The title page and contents should be cross-referenced to the report by page numbering. This is often forgotten, which then makes subsequent referrals more difficult to communicate.

2) The introduction is firstly a statement of the problem. If the report sponsor is unfamiliar with the issue concerned it may contain a more lengthy explanation to illustrate understanding of the problem concerned. A simple introduction might state. "The objective of this report is to examine the stock control techniques operating in the warehouse and make recommendations for their improvement. The reason for this is the £10,000 stock loss discovered at our last quarterly stock take."

3) The summary outlines the recommendations of the report and the estimated savings from the recommended action. It should be brief, since its purpose is to summarise the main points of the body of the report. Senior managers rarely have time to read all the documents laid on their desks, A good summary of no more than one side of A4 paper written in inspiring and stimulating terms will at least stand a better chance of being read. Once read, it should motivate the reader to read the whole report.

4) The present situation outlines in detail the present methods used. This should show understanding of the present position in the context of the whole and include a detailed analysis.

5) The analysis should clearly set out your explanation of the problem and its specific causes.

6) Recommendations are based upon an understanding and examination of the present, the recommendations for improvements and changes. These should be reasoned and present alternatives for consideration.

7) Appendices. Diagrams and data should be placed in appendices at the end of the report. These should be numbered and referred to in the text as appropriate.

Final points on report writing

- Remember to gather the facts. This relies upon knowledge of the problem and what you are looking for, so ensure that your mission is clear from the start.

- Next, analyse those facts. Try to be as objective as possible and avoid prejudice and preconceived ideas.

- Once you begin to write, present the facts accurately and as fairly as possible avoiding any slant.

- Write in short paragraphs, as this will appear more attractive to the eyes and easier to read. Layout is vital; blank paper is often as important as print. Use the KISS rule (Keep it Short and Simple) with:

  - Short sentences (fewer than 20 words) and don't repeat yourself. If is often useful to produce a draft and edit it for a final version.

  - Simple words, short words, no jargon. If initials or abbreviations are to be used, explain them fully first

  - Short paragraphs.

- Make recommendations stand out. Include recommendations in a summary as well as the text, and then they should be clear enough.

- Finally, check the report thoroughly before it is issued. Proof reading is vital to the impact of a report. Many senior managers will not read sloppily presented reports, and inaccuracies will at the very least detract and distract from the content of a report.

The object of a report is to improve the business by highlighting and solving a problem, or by raising standards and improving methods. To achieve this, then agreement must be obtained to put the recommendations into effect.

Presentation of an effective report is thus vital to achieving this end.

If no action is taken, the effort of producing the report is wasted, but worse, the opportunity to improve the business is lost.

Meetings

Meetings are frequently misused or badly organised and often result in confusion, lack of firm decisions and frustration. There are a number of different types of meeting, each involving a different role for the chairman, as follows:

- A formal meeting with strict procedures (the chairman's function is control).

- A meeting with the sole purpose of disseminating information (the chairman ensures all goes smoothly).

- A meeting where questions are encouraged and answered (the chairman ensures order, repeats the question for all to hear and selects which speaker is to answer, if there is a panel).

- Joint consultation (here the chairman must ensure that both sides get an equal hearing).

- Meetings to generate ideas, solve a problem, or make a decision (here the chairman still has some function of control, but needs discussion leading techniques to draw out all ideas and contributions).

- Brainstorming meetings to generate ideas (here the chairman is largely passive). A group gets together to discuss a project or problem and all ideas are encouraged, however wild. There are three stages: a warming up session on a light-hearted topic; the session itself; and a slightly more rational session to select about six ideas for further evaluation. The purpose of brainstorming is to generate ideas and creative thinking without the usual constraints

Preparing to lead a meeting

Step 1) Make an Outline.

- Determine the objectives: what do you wish to cover?
- Prepare a detailed discussion outline: how many aspects of the topic do you wish to discuss?
- How much total time is available?
- List points to be stressed: where will emphasis be placed?
- Plan the schedule: estimate the time to be spent on each aspect.
- Decide who should attend
- Decide what paperwork will be circulated at the meeting or in advance of the meeting

Step 2) Plan the Approach.

- What to say, how to say it, and how to approach the topic.

Step 3) Invite attendees

- Invite only those who must be there

- Prepare and circulate the agenda; this should be simple, clear, and timed.

Step 4) Have Everything Ready

- Make sure all necessary material and equipment are to hand.
- Make sure all members of the group have pencils, paper, etc., as necessary.

Step 5) Arrange the Meeting Room

- Make everyone comfortable
- Ensure that members are seated so that all can see and hear
- Look at ventilation, lighting, etc.

Conducting a meeting

Step 1) Open the Session on time

- Review background.
- Announce topic and objectives, briefly and concisely.
- Define procedure
- Open the first item on the agenda and lead into discussion smoothly and logically.

Step 2) Conduct the Discussion

- Encourage participation, use questions to get pooling of ideas, exchange of experiences, to draw out shy members.

- Control the discussion but stay in the background; prevent monopolisation by individual members, distribute questions evenly and avoid bias.
- Keep the discussion moving and on the subject/agenda; use questions to provoke thought and discussion; handle irrelevancies tactfully.
- Summarise frequently.

Step 4) Summarise the Meeting

- Point out highlights such as new ideas, experiences gained.
- Arrive at conclusions or solutions – what has been accomplished?
- Recap on who will take what action.
- End on a high note.
- Close on time.

Step 5) Follow Up – for example, it may be a good idea to issue a memo to confirm the findings and act as a checklist.

Meeting attendees

Step 1) Before the meeting

- Is the purpose clear?
- Did you receive the agenda, papers in time?
- Plan your participation

Step 2) During the meeting

- Did it start on time?
- Were the issues explained?

- Did everyone have a chance to contribute?
- Were summaries made?
- Were action points clear?
- Did it finish on time?

Step 3) After the meeting

- Was the agenda logical?
- Was enough time allowed?
- Was the meeting worthwhile?

Conclusion

In the introduction we highlighted several areas that managers can work on to improve productivity. These are shown again below with a link, (in brackets), to the appropriate Business Toolkit.

- Insufficient planning and control (see the Systems Thinking Toolkit)
- Inadequate supervision (see the Team Management Toolkit)
- Poor morale (see the Motivation Toolkit)
- Inappropriate people development (see the Developing People toolkit)
- IT related problems (included in the Systems Thinking Toolkit)
- Ineffective communication (dealt with in this Communication Toolkit)
- Poor Human Resources Management procedures (see the Human Resources Toolkit)
- Poor customer service (see the Customer Service Toolkit)
- Poor training/learning for specific skills and procedures (see the Learning Toolkit)

Readers are encouraged to take advantage of the complete list of toolkits, which complement each other to provide a comprehensive portfolio of concise pocket guides to improved personal and business performance.